To Hailey —
With lots of LOVE ♡
from Mom and Dad!
Keep sharing your LOVE
of learning!

Best wishes,

Paola Schmeer
3/2018

My Maddy, My Daddy

SECOND EDITION

by Rodo Sofranac

Illustrated by Kent Looft

Grammy Knows Books™

Library of Congress Control Number - 2016909997

ISBN: 978-0-9975685-4-7

Published by Grammy Knows Books, LLC
9622 North 24th Street
Phoenix, Arizona 85028-4608

Telephone: 602-992-5547
Email: grammyknowsbooks@gmail.com

Printed in the United States of America

Dedication

To all dads and their daughters,
as well as all parents and their
children.

Special thanks to Maddy for
helping to make this book come
to life.

Other books by Rodo:

Polly and the Peaputts
Polly and the Peaputts Pull Together
Polly and the Peaputts On The Move

I love my Maddy, because she teaches me so many new things.

I love my Daddy, because he teaches me so many new things.

"The colors of
the rainbow spell
ROY G. BIV...

Red, Orange,
Yellow, Green,
Blue, Indigo,
and Violet."

I love my Maddy, because she has great friends.

"This is Kai.
He's from
Hawai'i."

I love my Daddy, because he treats my friends like family.

I love my Maddy, because she is a great talker.

"Who was
the last one in
the bathroom?

The seat is
up again!

I bet it's one
of the boys!!"

I love my Daddy, because he is a great listener.

I love my
Daddy, because
he really
needs me.

"Maddy,
I need that
rechargeable
energy
hug!"

I love my Maddy, because she lifts my spirits and calms my temper.

I love my
Daddy
because
he cheers
me up
when
I'm down.

I love my Maddy, because
she really believes in me.

"Thank you for teaching me
about trust and faith."

I love my Daddy, because
he really believes in me.

"I may not always love what
you do, but I always love you!"

I love my Maddy, because she, her sister, and brothers are real examples of the love I share with my wife.

"I love my family!"

I love my Daddy, because he picked Mom, and loves her so much.

"I love you, Susan."

Bios

Rodo Sofranac, Author

Rodo Sofranac is not only Maddy's daddy, but of three more loving kids. He's also been an uncle, granddad, mentor, tormentor, deputy dad, and Mr. Nice Guy to lots of other great kids. Rodo now shares his love with Maddy across thousands of miles of desert and ocean, proving once again that time and distance can't separate love.

A MESSAGE FROM MADDY

Maddy's daddy's loving guidance continues to help her learn and grow to live radiantly and influence others, as well. She still loves enjoying and sharing his figs with friends! ALOHA!

Kent Looft, Illustrator

Kent spent most of his childhood tramping about the citrus groves and lakes of Southern California. He attended Mount San Antonio State College and Art Center College, Los Angeles with a Bachelors of Arts in Advertising Design and Illustration. During college, he worked part-time producing more than 1000 watercolor portraits at the Disney theme park, Anaheim, CA.

Kent has received regional and national awards including, the SBA National Poster Design Comission in Washington D.C., The American Catalog Design Awards, NY, Arizona Festival Awards for poster illustration. Kent's paintings and sculpture work has been shown at the Chandler Vision Gallery and The Shermer Art Center, Phoenix.

Kent and his wife, Gracie, live in Chandler, Arizona. Email: klooft@gmail.com

This book is dedicated to our noble and cherished fathers, John H. Kinney, Jr. and Fred C. Stolle. You were our kings when we were little princesses and you still rule! You taught us life was an adventure and have energetically led the way for us. Thank you for a lifetime of example, encouragement, and support. We love you!

And again to our five princesses, may you find Him in every tangled adventure . . .

J.Y. and J.J.

Dedicated to my father . . .

O.A.

ZONDERKIDZ

Princess Charity's Courageous Heart

Copyright © 2012 by Jeanna Young and Jacqueline Johnson
Illustrations © 2012 by Omar Aranda

Requests for information should be addressed to:
Zonderkidz, Grand Rapids, Michigan 49530

Library of Congress Cataloging-in-Publication Data

Young, Jeanna Stolle, 1968-
    Princess Charity's courageous heart / by Jeanna Young and Jacqueline
Johnson; illustrated by Omar Aranda.
        p.   cm.
    Summary: When adventurous young Princess Charity defies her father's
orders and rides into a neighboring kingdom, she sees a boy fall from his horse,
watches others pass him by, and finally goes to help him herself in this version
of the parable of the Good Samaritan. Includes note about the parable and its
meaning for children.
    ISBN 978-0-310-72701-9 (hardcover)
    [1. Princesses—Fiction. 2. Christian life—Fiction. 3. Parbles]. I. Young, Jeanna
Stolle, 1968- II. Aranda, Omar, ill. III. Title.
PZ7.J63214Pj 2012
[E]—dc23   2011024864

Editor: Mary Hassinger
Art direction and design: Kris Nelson and Mary pat Pino

Printed in China

The Princess Parables

Princess Charity's
Courageous Heart

WRITTEN BY **Jeanna Young** & **Jacqueline Johnson**
ILLUSTRATED BY **Omar Aranda**

ZONDERVAN.com/
AUTHORTRACKER
follow your favorite authors

Once upon a time, in a magnificent castle perched high on a hill above the sea, there lived five princesses. Their names were Joy, Grace, Faith, Hope, and Charity. They were blessed to be the daughters of the king.

This is the story of Princess Charity, the youngest of the five sisters. When she smiles, her emerald eyes sparkle with fun and a hint of mischief. She is the most fearless of the sisters and can often be found climbing trees, or chasing foxes across the meadow. She often wears riding boots and knickers under her frilly gown anticipating a daring adventure . . .

One day as Princess Charity finished grooming her horse, Daisy, a trusted servant approached her.

"Is it fitting for a princess to be in the stables cleaning and caring for the animals?" he asked. "Would your father approve of this and your trips near the border of Sir Richard's land? Your sisters are always busy with royal responsibilities in the castle."

"But this is my favorite place in the kingdom," Princess Charity respectfully replied, hugging Daisy's neck. "And I REALLY love my adventures!"

That night the king told grand stories of his latest travels and daring deeds while the girls listened intently. Princess Charity thought to herself how one day she wanted to be a courageous knight and go out into the unknown world.

"Daddy, why aren't we allowed to go beyond the Weeping Woodlands?" she interrupted.

The king hesitated, and then sternly replied, "Charity, I have told you before, our neighbor, Sir Richard, has decided to guard his borders. You are not allowed on his land. Is that understood, girls?"

All the princesses nodded … except for Princess Charity.

That night Charity dreamed of adventure and exploration. The next morning, before her sisters awoke, she left a note saying she had gone riding and would be back after lunch. Then she went out to the stable to saddle Daisy for a ride.

Charity galloped through the countryside and up to Monument Hill to look out over the kingdom. She remembered what her father had said about not crossing the border. But surely she could look down by the creek that divided Sir Richard's land from her father's.

While eating her picnic lunch, Princess Charity watched a young boy racing a horse and buggy along the dirt path that followed the creek. He was so close to Sir Richard's side! *He is going much too fast,* she thought.

Just then, his horse buggy's wheel hit a rock. The boy went flying through the air, landing motionless in a ditch. Princess Charity jumped to her feet with a muffled cry and whispered a prayer, "How can we help this hurting boy, God?"

Princess Charity looked for someone to come to the boy's rescue. In the distance, she saw a nobleman's coach speeding down the path.

"Oh, good, Daisy. Here comes help!" she sighed with relief. However, the nobleman's coach passed by with only a short pause where the boy lay. *Oh, no!* Princess Charity thought in distress. *They didn't stop!*

Princess Charity wasted no time. She jumped on Daisy and rode down to the edge of the creek. As she approached, she saw a group of Sir Richard's soldiers charging down the path. Charity hid behind some boulders with a clear view of the boy.

"Oh, thank you, Lord!" she breathed "Surely, *they* will stop!" But, just as the nobleman had done, the soldiers whisked by without even a glance at the hurt boy.

"Daisy, THAT'S IT! I must rescue him!" Princess Charity declared overcome with compassion. "But he is so close to Sir Richard's border. What if the soldiers return?"

After looking both ways, Charity and Daisy bolted from behind the rocks. She attached the cart to Daisy and put the wounded boy into the buggy. She gently wiped his face, then wasting no time, headed back to the castle.

Seeing Princess Charity in the distance, Princess Hope and her sisters ran to meet her at the gate.

"Where have you been?" "Who is this?" "Where did you find him?" "How did he get hurt?" each princess asked Charity.

"I don't know who he is! But we must help him," Princess Charity answered. Quickly, they moved him into the castle. Servants gathered around to help the princesses with the boy.

After hearing the news from the groomsman, the king found Charity outside the guest room and asked, "Charity, where were you today?"

"Daddy, I went riding … passed the Weeping Woodlands … up to Monument Hill … I saw this boy get hurt! He was so close to Sir Richard's border and I watched as others passed him by without stopping to help!" she stammered while her sisters gasped. "I had to help him and so I brought him back here."

Suddenly, they heard loud voices and clanging swords. Before the king could say a word, he was summoned to the entrance of the castle.

The king found the servants fretting as soldiers burst into the Grand Hall. Sir Richard was announced and the king went to greet him.

"Do you have my son?" Sir Richard thundered.

"Your son?" the king repeated.

"Yes, he was seen being brought here by one of your daughters. My soldiers were looking for him because he ran away. They did not recognize him as the boy in the ditch."

Turning to the girls, Sir Richard implored, "Which one of you girls saved my son?"

Slowly, Princess Charity stepped forward.

Taking her hand, Sir Richard begged, "How can I ever repay you?"

With no thought for herself, Princess Charity requested peace between the two kingdoms. Sir Richard quickly accepted. Days later his son, Jack, was well enough to go home. He promised to return to ride with Princess Charity another day.

As they watched him ride away, the king smiled, turned to Princess Charity, and said, "Your heart was kind and full of mercy for this young boy. I am so proud of you! Not only is he safe and well, but peace has returned between our two kingdoms." Taking her hand in his, he added, "And because of your courage, my sweet one, we have all been blessed with new friends."

Parable Thoughts

I am Princess Charity. My name means "giving, kindness, and brotherly love." Even though I want to be lion-hearted and adventurous, I may not always make the right decisions. My father always helps me see that showing love and mercy for those who are hurting and reaching out to help them is real charity-in-action. When I think back on my daring adventure to rescue Jack, I was frightened and unsure of what to do. In the end, I chose the charitable action and risked myself to save Jack. Not thinking I would receive anything in return, I was rewarded with peace between our kingdom and Sir Richard's . . . and a new friend!

This story reminds me of a true story my sisters read to me out of the Bible. You can find it in Luke 10:30–37. Jesus tells us how to be giving and kind, investing whatever we have to help those in need. This is true charity and our calling!

Jesus replied, "A man was going down from Jerusalem to Jericho. Robbers attacked him. They stripped off his clothes and beat him. Then they went away, leaving him almost dead. A priest happened to be going down that same road. When he saw the man, he passed by on the other side. A Levite also came by. When he saw the man, he passed by on the other side too.

But a Samaritan came to the place where the man was. When he saw the man, he felt sorry for him. He went to him, poured olive oil and wine on his wounds and bandaged them. Then he put the man on his own donkey. He took him to an inn and took care of him. The next day he took out two silver coins. He gave them to the owner of the inn. 'Take care of him,' he said. 'When I return, I will pay you back for any extra expense you may have.'"

"Which of the three do you think was a neighbor to the man who was attacked by robbers?"

The authority on the law replied, "The one who felt sorry for him."

Jesus told him, "Go and do as he did."

Luke 10:30–37 (NIrV)